Salt Water

Rhian Gallagher

Salt Water Creek

ENITHARMON PRESS

First published in 2003
by the Enitharmon Press
26B Caversham Road
London NW5 2DU

www.enitharmon.co.uk

Distributed in the UK by
Central Books
99 Wallis Road
London E9 5LN

Distributed in the USA and Canada
by Dufour Editions Inc.
PO Box 7, Chester Springs
PA 19425, USA

ISBN 1 900564 38 6

Enitharmon Press gratefully acknowledges the
financial support of Arts Council England

British Library Cataloguing-in-Publication Data.
A catalogue record for this book is available
from the British Library.

Typeset in Bembo by Servis Filmsetting Ltd
and printed in England by
Antony Rowe Ltd

ACKNOWLEDGEMENTS

Thanks to the editors of the following magazines and anthologies in which some of these poems have appeared: *Poetry Review, London Magazine, Ambit, Poetry Wales, Stand, Poetry London, The Rialto, Sport, Landfall, The Independent on Sunday, Love Shook My Senses: Lesbian Love Poems* (Women's Press, 1998), *The Poetry Business Anthology 1994, The Daily Telegraph Arvon International Poetry Competition Anthology 2000*.

Thanks also to The Poetry School and London Arts Board for the opportunity to participate in the pilot Mentoring Scheme. I'm indebted to my mentor, Carol Rumens, for her helpful response to my work throughout that year.

My gratitude to Nora Flaherty, Catherine Lamb, Jane Duran, and Alison Slienger for reading versions of this collection and for their valuable suggestions and comments.

For Mum and Dad
In Memory

CONTENTS

Where paddocks end, and the wind's
no longer broken by the pines . . .
Where sea happens to the island, grey
    slack of the beach between.
    The wind-driven sea,
the wild and unprotected light.

Scooped out clay loam, tear-ridged
rain-trails
    and the path crooked.
Years since I came this way,
came back from England this thaw season
– lupin flower and toothed geranium.

Wind that rocks all shadows, brings
dust from foothills, birds from far
shores. And either side of rail lines
    low curling through sea grasses
wind like a body turning beneath sheets
    sounds like 'taper,' 'bevel'
briney-gathers touch upon my skin

one layer after another –
an empty shore drained of colour,
blue tiles peeling
to the wave's white tinge.
With each roller's break
    burnt foam
tonnage of voice in the undertow
makes a place in my head
like floating or screaming
the Pacific
– black coals of tree washed back,
gulls spooling
the wrought blue, home, from England.

BACKYARD

When my father murdered the chickens
I'd run across the open ground, taking cover.
Boundary lines of wire and wind-battered cherry trees.

Inside the macrocarpa was a cave,
bits of sunlight on the needles.
The chickens danced without their heads,
their chook-blood gushing as if they were on fire.

I buried treasure in a tin,
bottle-glass and china.

There were hollows and pockets in the grass.
I lay on my side, listening
for a train or a river, wanting to go.

Because of the winds
there was always someone looking
for someone at the top of their voice

even as dusk drew squiggly lines
round the old pear tree
and sparrows dropped to poles and wires
going over the day in a song

there was still an animal, beyond the boundary,
bellowing across the big ground for its love.

chook is kiwi-slang for chicken

THE NIGHT SHE LEFT

My father moved as if he'd lost his place
and then sat down; turned up his hands
that rested on his knees, and looked into them
as if they were in question.
We had not heard their voices rise.
Nothing visible was broken.
The back door opened. Closed.

I see her walk, walking out,
down the slope past windbreak pines
– their tall darkness shifting with creak, ache, sigh.
Paddocks crossed by day grew
and lost their green without the sun,
fences dropped as shadows on the land
– acres under dark went wide and deep.
He didn't follow. She didn't stop
but turned for the road to the sea.

How far did she go, after the road,
into the blackness on the stones of the beach below?
We'll never know – the rough clod bank
then rocks and knots of lupin before
the plume and spree of foam, the breaking sea.
Her footing lost, or hesitating. Her meaning
to go on that brought her back.
The wind filling her mouth shapeless
as tears. Unspoken – that night in all their years.

I rolled on and off the bunk.
My mother hung our coats on hangers,
everything went sideways.
I stretched my legs up
and clamped my feet to the ceiling.
Tea broke over the cup's lip
– we were out at sea.

Decks below the engines gurgled
in their grease, after that there was a skin
of metal and rivets that kept us from the water.
The water was dark, live, and so deep
that if you fell into it you would fall
and fall passing fish with neon eyes
– it would take days to reach the end.

My mother said 'get into your pyjamas
and brush your teeth' like it was home
– but no land was in view. It was all sea.
The water in my body
swished to and fro like the tea.

So in the morning I was amazed
that we'd made it through the night.
I put my face to the porthole
to thank the fish and water for our lives
but a wave, coming sideways,
eyed me with its hollow. This was the sea.
It could swallow the whole ferry if it wanted to.

'Breakfast' my mother was saying, her voice
came from far away, everything balanced on a tray.

I could be here for hours, learning how to live with myself,
treading carefully because of all the broken glass.

The gulls zoning in on clippings, the sound
they made was like clippings. The sea never emptied.
There was a speed of cloud.

Climbing round torn-open cars I touched each crash
on the way, like it meant something.

Swinging through the old Ford's windscreen
I thought of Doctor Who's telephone box.
Amid clouds of smoke and smells of rust

I pushed what levers there were and pumped the pedals.
When nothing worked I leant back
against raw springs and waited.

FIND A PARTNER

Our teacher is waltzing across the lawn with Linda.
An extension cord loops from the window,
crosses the rose-beds. The music crackles

as if on waves from England.
'Watch my feet,' he shouts
as he circles the fire bush

brushing the strawberry tree. Linda looks airborne.
Our ballroom has a sky-blue roof, a tractor
ploughing across the horizon,
roses peel to the sun

as piano launches anew, crossing a sea of static
a rise and a fall and a boy
with a grip on my arm as if it were a baseball bat.
The feeling of being inside my body
arrives with this news – it's going to be difficult.

RIDING PILLION

We go to the high country –
the station farm and the farm-bike
which has forks like a horse's flanks

you take your death-dare and me
onto the trail with this
machine and its seven hundred and
fifty horses between your thighs

the day could have been otherwise
to this, there's a kind of bliss
high up in these hills
the wild and the quiet in one

but you want
nothing but speed
winding up the throttle
until the chasm
where I scream

the machine lifts
into the air
and for a moment we
balance there, over the void
till the rear wheel kisses
the edge and we land.

You are driving us
into the mountains now –
you are my man
I hold on as tight as I can.

PORTRAIT OF A YOUNG PRINCESS

Master of Moulins

How long summer lies on those hills
and behind those hills, land to land.
The power of a window. His.

Back turned to light,
I pass to an interior of coolness
to stand in his arc, fitted with shadow.
I learn what it is to be

vividly portrayed. My hair under a weight
of brocade where no breeze could
loose a strand, or taste. The rich
dress I wear — red, trimmed
at the clavicle and wrist. Two petals

and a stamen at my throat.
I feed the devotion between my fingers,
fifteen mysteries on a knotted cord.

What did I ask you, water of no-going,
sluggish as a trough, forsaken
grey-song trundling round the town's back?

Beyond you roads lay, the sea
decked with harbour, freighters from Russia
leashed to the port.

I'd run through paddocks
on the scent of a climate change,
skirting the home radar, five miles out.

I was a cargo,
ready to weigh on a good tide.
Or be swept by the rails
with my ear to the pulse, tick-tack of journey
inside the snake of a train.

You were my first border, channel to be crossed,
like all water you had no ties.
I looked into the halt of you, torpid
and speechless, while the reeds and the wind
made sad-worded songs.

The wavering found me
on the greasy mud of your side,
caught in a slip between worlds
where the woollen mill cast its dyes
and the salt marsh oozed.

A heron broke its own stillness,
wings turning to smoke as it rose.
The man in the petrol station called home.

I stalled among the day weeds, dock and thistle,
under a cloud, awaiting my father
with all that the water said, a water
of no ilk, paler than darkness.

Ours is the quiet trade,
the trowel in my hand, plaster
on the trowel, the intimate relationship
as I glide up the seams.

The mix is live, a wetness
that sounds back along my arm
for a span and then dies.
The trowel stalls, the clog and stick
of attachment till I'm in the grip of the wall.

The site itself heaves and bangs,
drills go off. Blokes shout
like hands on deck
crossing the noise of big sea

while John seems to float above me
up on the scaffold, his head craned,
a man working backwards like Michelangelo.
His breath comes out with a small slap
at the end of each stroke, his body set on a slope,
a marriage of arm and eagle's eye.

The ceiling takes shape.
John winks down at me cheekily
back-dropped by this new inner-sky.

THE SCAFFOLD

The cat comes from nowhere, quiet
as a premonition, walking
on her toes in the gap where the window will go.
I'm on the outside, six floors up.
Siamese or Burmese, she pauses now
taking sun like an expert.

I bend for the wet sand mix
load up the trowel and aim it into the rough blank wall.
Last week a man plunged to his death.
The scaffold bounces and shakes like a dance floor.

Work being done in a hurry. Pavements crammed
with makeshift planks and poles. Cranes,
their long jib arms, glide
with girders above roof lines.

My mind pulling on slack.
When the cat runs the plank beside me
it's just as his mates said, not even time for a prayer,
my limbs freeze on the scaffold with its vacancy.

Her brisk, no fuss, doing-song
filled me with event. Just going to town,
lining clothes up on the bed –
the way she paused over a scarf's knot
and moons on nails and gave me scent

as if I weren't small and seven but tall, tall
enough for long words like *conspicuous*.
She gave me her time. The weight
and coolness of blue glass against skin,
my first beads not to pray with. She gave me
the OK like flight control giving clearance
for take-off. The long echo of her heels
hitting a high note on pavement.

THE WHARF

The shed side of town where rail lines converged
and a pointsman lowered and raised a wooden arm,
I breathed the oily air of passage, the sun
strobing off silos, and that indifference
that comes into my head at the moment
of departure, perhaps an inherited scent,
nosegays of immigration, the big lifting-up-of-your-life
borne to me on a chemical breeze, gun-metal
of a loading crane – cargoes. Those room-sized
corrugated containers, unmarked dry goods,
that blankness again, troubling
and longing like the place, loading
unloading – the very idea
of trading with the world.

I wasn't leaving. I was just walking under shadows
of the big ships that had stabled in the port,
water sluicing from their sides. I could hear them
ticking over, hear them strain on their ropes
their wider-than-my-arm ropes
skewered in knots as large as my head.
There was a sea-growth on everything: salt-scoured rusting,
barnacles on the tree-sides of the wharf, and those ropes,
with a catch of bladder weed and bull kelp.
The feeling of being not quite on land, the wharf
sleepers stained with the tar of old rail-lines,
keeping solid yet stationed in the drift.

Our Dead

On their anniversaries, on all the holy days
that wheeled through each year, we'd go.
My father made a job of it, cutting
grass, cleaning the stones – grandmother,
grandfather, my mother's sister, my own
sister, all in the earth without a window.
My mother brought flowers,
sought out the single tap and filled the jars.

When everything we'd come to do was done,
in that pause, time opened inside my head
because our dead were dead forever – a space
that went from stone to earth, from earth to air,
from air to sky and blue beyond that blue.

Whatever point I got to there was more –
forever. I'd blink to have the grass back at my feet.
I'd keep a solemn, grown-up face –
our dead were dead and gone.

Down in the main street
where the winds smell of crop and sea
blowing hot, blowing cold
the day finds me – back home
dazed by the light.

Things that put the place on the map:
concrete power poles, macaroni
and a race horse called Phar Lap.
The single main street joins to Highway One
north, south – you can hear
the strangers leaving – it's a straight run.

Large as ever, the plains
peel off the boundary, back to hills.
Paddocks square up to each other.
I can smell that space on street corners
– the farmers' broad Fords nose from carparks,
painted with the dust of tertiary roads.

Spear leaves of cabbage trees
edged on the wind,
there's a port for the grain and meat
and a bay for summer, and the wind
rumbles through most days with discontent or hunger.

I walk down the aisle
of Whitcoulls where Aunt Trish served.
She kept small change in her pocket,
called up to her boss that she's just stepping
out for a coffee – I go where we would have gone.
I sit in May's Milk Bar and the town
sits about me as if it had never been far.

THE BASILICA

Big bowl at sky-level, towering
the town, visible beyond the boundary,
radiating at so many miles distant
boom, boom, heavy as Rome, masonry
with the reach of a rock formation.

The avenue shook. Bells clapped,
their iron tongues racketing
stripped Sunday of its sleep-filled air,
rung down on me like a warning.
The tall doors swung like a rock face opening.

Herded in, the family made a procession,
God at his watch, a big chill roving
the tiled expanse – this was no one's home.
All our faces turning up to pray
– his ear was in our souls
listening for a footstep making stray.

MY FATHER

He would square up like a captain,
as if some huge parade hinged on his posture
and he bolted himself in
to where he thought the centre was.
He held up the wind, the sun wouldn't dare
shift an inch, the very air seemed to poise
on his shoulders. His halt was enormous
– every cell organised into one
breath-taking feat of readiness.

Set up in the backyard with his church-going suit on,
or in his work gear under the pear tree.
I still don't know when that man left
but in this frame my mother holds the camera
still wanting to give him the pleasure.
A head and shoulders shot, close up
yet her captain is small and far away.

I can see my mother looking
through the viewfinder, smiling encouragement.
And because my father hasn't left completely
but is past the onset (his memory falling like a sea wall,
his mind floating over a district of names)
he struggles toward her, towards the ceremony.
His smile is almost beaten, almost blank.

Amaryllis

It came above the water line, bottle-green
into the light, among the curtains and the lamps.
She told me how it started,
how she'd turned it to the clock of the sun

whose rays across the window
shifted through her day like a tide.
Heady as moon-rise unloading in a room of sickness.
A room whose surfaces keeled under bric-à-brac
– things she'd kept not knowing why –
the ghost of someone else's heirlooms.
Low tones of mothballs from the drawers,

silks she wouldn't touch again.
A coming magnified against the heavy furniture,
the flesh thick stem softly blowing out its flower.
She'd had the quick step of a dancer;
I thought of her lovers, her poise,

as the illness set her back again.
Bedroom days under dressings of lanolin,
a season breathed around the room.
Her wrists, her ankles – those fine bones –

and the way her breasts still cupped into a V,
defiant among bedsores.
Years later in a bar below the street, lonely
and single, there was that flower
lighting a corner above the seated crowd,

straightening its back to me.
And something I had to hear in her voice
to believe, when it came a second time,
she'd said the whiteness was like a liturgy,
like a wedding without regret.

A Winter's Room

The score of a song on the walls of a winter's room,
a fox waiting on grass, the lilacs dark and empty.
We heard the train on tracks behind the trees
and then the bells of evensong, the ropes undone,
it was early and already night had come.

Reaching for you was to hear the light expand
till high on the frosted ceiling of the city
the birds that had not returned
were singing. Your breasts lifting beneath my lips,
mist torn against the blue depths of winter,
your touch erasing, divining,
climbing true home as if it were a wave
as if it were a tender fall of foam, we held
and the colours ran.
A soft voice in the wind:
your 'yes' that warmed the winter through.

The Away Days

I lie on the rocks at the end of the strand
and listen to waves work up the reef.
The cool–weather waters of the Atlantic
going all the way to Canada.

Back on this coast, the mountains have warmed
– each dip of their blues joins to a rise.
I think of her, in that drifting way,
making a pillow with my arms, breathing
over my wrist, over the white rooftops of barnacles.

Bees scout the kelp beds,
wings of a butterfly pulse on the wind.
I have the last time inside my head.
No phone or post. It's a different kind of contact
coming through. The tallness of her, the wave length.

CYCLE ROUTE

It's a small country,
a kind of province below tower blocks
with nettles and weeds and something like the idea of trees
holding on to the light. Ricket-bone stems.

The narrowing has made the life intense –
wire fenced, walled, the surround land loaded
with scrap yard, DIY warehouse, and waste transfer-station.

When the days were still good with us
I imagined our way here just before dark.
Pillows of light lie on the water
I'm looking out to it now –

the Wandle widens
at its mouth before the Thames.
Everything we never did comes to me,
rambling and delighting, against the boundaries.

AFFAIR

I hardly know now why we came
there were some people she knew here
not in her married life but on the outskirts
where she went by her first name.
Along the pebbles small groups sat
sealed in their clothes, looking out
on a churning cabbage-coloured sea.
Her catwalk stride, oozing indifference,
held me in sway. Like the waves
she could toy with an end and then come back,
her face unset, her eyes the eyes of a lover
– I was bound in the net of that gaze.

When I lost her for a moment out on the pier
it was like the other side of our affair.
I could hear the rain being prepared, clouds
tightening their salts. The bellowing depths.

I listened out for the sound, the red
drawl of her car. The street vibrated
with a thousand mirrors, rain
tapping the roof like small glass.
As a prayer called across evening
young men paced past, their side-locks
bouncing beneath dark brims.

The rain falling off the rim of umbrellas,
droplets swelling on the tips of leaves.
The beautiful litter of water.

When she did not come, there was no stillness
so I walked wet-stippled pavements
till the silence caught up with me.
How vast and small the city was,
her on the other side of it
joined by a sky of blanket-grey,
yet the distance was everything.

I cannot know where she is now.
Always suspended, mid-flight
she sat on the edge of chairs, keys in hand.
Her futures twitched, her other life elsewhere,
perfume like breath left on the air.

There are streets that remember her,
each pavement with another just below the surface.
No sound comes yet I'm ready to hear her,
her going-away footsteps, between buildings.
The silence that draws after,
succinct as a knife-edge. Her precision.

SEASIDE

We are all here, sitting on the pavement drinking beer.
That kid, who is almost a relation,
sucking on her stick of Brighton rock.
As we pass the postcard along the line
oldest brother writes 'I've just come along
for the ride'. Youngest brother scrawls 'Hi mum,
a word from your son who never writes.'

I sit between them linking arms for the snap.
She'll want a print. After years, and for once
in the same country, how having the same mother
can seem like a new fact – brothers,
looking like they just came down
from the high country, ready to put their hands
to anything: bouncing on the end of a bungy,
building a house. But it's true, she taught us
all how to swim out in the sea,
we pick up the story just beyond the break-line.
From Caroline Bay with its nikau palms to Hove
– the bathing chalets looking like outhouses built out back
of an Opihi bach. The sunlight unsteady, the beach stony.

Only flickers of home then, below the jazzy roofline
along the Esplanade when Palace Pier lights come on
making us all hungry. And on the motorway back
to London when the car goes ropy, and we know
if we stop the whole thing will likely die –
as if this is where the family's always been as we sing,
sing like hell for all the lights to turn green.

---

bach: Kiwi term (pronounced 'batch') for a holiday home, these days ranging from
a shed to a palatial residence, most often built by a lake, a river or the sea.

COTTAGE AT DRUMLIDRIGE

I tread lightly around the ruins,
solid stone on a soaked earth bed.
I tread as if I were trespassing,
as if the wind were wired
and the dead could be woken.

I draw the window in quietly
and watch the rain, feeling how
each wall is working back into the hill.
The stones like childhoods, letting go
their hold inside the rain.

Cows wade in the dark peat mud.
The brown earth extends
beyond folds of ashen heather
and furrows of the bog, a vantage point
that reaches to the strand –

the Atlantic. As if there were clues
that could come back off that sea,
rewinding his passage in slow motion.
As if the warm interior were still here
like an origin, my father
having a word in my ear.

LANDLADY

You are framed, looking out of the doorway
bric-à-brac stacks the stairwell.
When your aunts died their things moved in.
Boxes you never seem ready to unpack,
chairs, lampshades – homeless belongings.

The wind stumbles across the garden,
are there faces looking up from the ground?
The trees, pulling back and forth at the fence-lines,
under the sound of weight shifting
what is it you hear? The fronts of Poland?

Your father keeps to his chair in the heated back room,
holy cards propped against tablet bottles – the Pope,
the Sacred Heart. He was a mender of clocks
till his sight failed against the small pins and balances.

Poplars sway beyond you, foliage laid in like feathers.
The pear tree shoots go out pell-mell.
Cousins of cousins come by coach across Europe,
long journeys fill the rooms, brown roads,
the colour of gunmetal.

The strong house has started to fail.
Your face gaunt, you carry the winters there.
Broken roof tiles, gutters that are sieves in the rain.
Unwilling keeper – observing all the holy days,
the smell of beet soup rising through the rooms
cloudy as a nocturne.

Old clocks make a wall, their faces no longer moving.
And now it is spring, the wind showers blossom,
a touch that's light and fleeting as breath.
The garden tingles, and the doorway exhausts you.

THE QUIET PLACE

I cannot set a colour against it
or rest it on my knee.
The sound of a glove pulled on a hand,
amber, through a glass, through a tapestry,
the quiet place opens like water.
As I look into greyness, as the children
look under the stones for the light,
as the tongue of the bells mid-week
calls to a ship or a wedding.
The quiet place.
After the song ends,
after the chemistry – a cooling sky.
As if I were listening to miles
slowly. It's where I outstay my time,
the small boat tied,
the mother ship anchored in the bay.

They are the same colour as the deer.
The deer drift like séance voices
over the dead bracken.
I hold my hand
against the bark
and think of my father's face
drinking in the winter light.
Countries away,
muffled in cloud
I try to keep the picture of him moving.
His wading stride,
crossing a paddock
in hobnail boots.
Steady as these boughs,
just leaning into the wind
as if everlasting.

BURIAL

The shovels stood in a sticky underbelly of earth
as we stepped from the sidelines for him,
peeling our jackets, the boys loosening their ties.
Soon there was clay on our church-going gear
and his voice coming out of our childhood
coaching us to put our backs into it.
Flowers and fine words had never touched the man
like work, grunts behind a shovel's bite,
the clean sound of clods as we heaved them in. Digging,
we bowed in memory of his stooped solid shape.
The dark damp weight of earth,
a provision, a very last word.

My Father's Faith

We think of him as here
along the home-stretch of the cemetery.
In today's deserted quiet
it's as if I'm landscaping him in,
back from inland hills, inside the fence-line
where marcrocarpas, plied by the south beach wind,
bend and right themselves.

Yet the stone is for us now, marker
on this newly muddled earth
with its top side of clay that the rains will settle.

Unlike him, I believe without any sureness.
But if there's marriage of a good heart to promised heaven
he should be miles from here by now,
in that backyard of paradise,
chopping the wood, no doubt, and feeding the animals.

SAN MINIATO

The boys on the bridge play dead in the heat
lounging on stone, their guitars laid aside.
Above them a breeze roves
fruit trees and vines earth on terraces of the slope.

From hilltop light into the church –
it feels like girlhood, stepping into the clutches
of a semidark. That uncertain temperature.

But as my eyes adjust, I'm stepping here
across a floor given over to colour, lions,
doves, and each month with its sign.
The monk on his own in a pew, bent to his beads
labouring in the calm. His earthy robe
against a tapestry of animals.

The colour, I would make it a religion.
As I step back into the day, it feels like a sound
carrying all over Florence, between the boys and the monk.
The Arno, a yellow thread, winding below.

LINEA

Moss and lichen of a thousand rains
come with me as I roll against the dark
my open hoops tangling into the interior

there are times when I step into line
and map my way against the solid
lifting into the canopy and then this
aspiration for a great height
leaves me and I swing out from kauri, beech,
from everything I thought I wanted.

A linea is a climbing, woody vine-like plant, plentiful in the bush in NZ

SHINE

When the back door and the front door opened
you could see right through the house
to sky at the far end –
the doors lined-up to make this corridor.
Every morning my mother got down
on her hands and knees
and polished the linoleum.
She pushed big rags around and sang
Danny Boy and *The Green Green Grass of Home.*
I helped, messing the words up
and sometimes, with my bum on a rag,
she would push me around like a boat.

Her work would come back to me
as I bathed her, knees of a penitent,
the swellings round each joint in her hands.
Five days into the coma there was the night
when her breathing calmed, to and fro,
I could feel her going, under the rhythm
beyond the room, across the plains
each paddock opening – she was so light.

The wind with its sound of doorways.
Somewhere at the end of the corridor
there was the morning sky, and the wind.
For days I will feel her there, housing and leaving.

CAROLINE BAY

The cloud clears, cliffs and ribs of jetty
edging out from the bay.

I crouch among driftwood, finger-reading
one piece and then another – furrow,
expanse, complex as a brow.
In the wet beneath, sand hoppers
jump and burrow like a gang, a single pulse.

Idling the wood in my hand, deciding
what to pack and what to leave
I step among tide wash – broken shells,
matted seagrass, kelp. The storm is over.
The wind gentles. Fronds of nikau palm unroll.

All day on the floor of her room
amid black bags, one blue shirt
lifted from the pile – that shade
along the sleeves, so much her

the way I can see her now, lifting her head
looking out to sea as if it were a chapel.

That blue that fits
the Pacific to the sky. How I am here
stopped by a line she has crossed. Alone.

MY BROTHERS' SUITS

They stand in the pose of altar boys, the first fifteen,
feet parted, weight drawn up. Team photos.
Collar and tie that they hardly ever wear, their eyes
steady on a moment directly in front of them.

A procession of ceremonies, from christening to confirmation,
in the air of the church surrounding them –
all the way back to grandfather laying the stone, burying
his overalls beneath the foundations.
Standing as men in the family have stood in rooms, in lines,
in the front row pew. Bodies squared beneath dark suits.

It's like nowhere when the grief finds them,
a tenor voice choked, shoulders crumbling.
My younger brother on a pub's steps in London after midnight,
crying against a mobile phone as if our mother's voice
were locked inside. My older brother swimming out beyond the raft
in the dead of winter, swimming against nothing, against the gap.

St Nicholas in St Ives/The Church of the Good Shepherd in Tekapo (NZ)

It's like the chapel of a pioneer. Compact
sea-weathered stone. I rest my back against the outer wall.

My mother once stood inside an evening's light,
the chapel's walls around her as rough and thick
as the wall that takes the weight along my spine.
Its window faced a lake. It stood alone
beyond the town and like this chapel on its hill
could transform the visitor into a pilgrim.
Walking the rocky path as if toward Mecca
or Lourdes, feeling the bow inside me.

I'm in the quiet now, looking out to sea
where evening's light is like a voice interpreting a dream.
The look of gravity and softness on her face
as she turned from the altar to the lake.
It was hard to say which was strongest in her,
a love of God, or the water that she loved
for its volume – an eternity of blue.

HOTEL ROOM

It's a room just off to the side of our lives,
newly emptied. Our small clutter
spills across polished surfaces as we fill the vacancy.
Half-emptied bags wear yesterday's flight tags,
voices come through the wall like a cloud.

As if we could stay indefinitely,
the room has no country.
Each of us slipping over lines with a touch.
All around are towers, window squares of light,
the city sounds, loading, unloading.
We draw the curtains on a night as wide as the Atlantic.

THE DOUBLE RAINBOW

All day the rainbows are being made
as we walk across boroughs, their tiny measures
gather in the stratosphere. Piebald cloud
then blue again, the water's invisible
rounding off the horizon – all we hear are the planes
as they bank into an altitude of departure.

It is her last day. The distances are growing
as we climb over tufts of heathland
and London unfolds. A spire lifts above trees
and then the lofty heights where the planes ride.

But the light has followed us, filling the sky in
between the cloud and we could not be closer –
arms linked under one umbrella as the first arc
completes across the pond, and with colours reversed
the second arc climbs beside the first.

We stand under their meeting, the light
and the rain finding each other –
the extraordinary beauty of rainbow to rainbow
and the dark band between them, part of the circumstances.

HER FACE

Not sleeping but with eyes closed,
a letting-go softness
blooming across her brow, her cheek.

My eyes are not enough,
my fingers lighten on her face
and it's like touching inside her
beyond myself and coming back
with a universe to be shaped
into that single word.

Even now as she brushes the footsteps of sleep
I know my voice could reach her
yet against any word from me
her face is complete.

They've just emerged, surrounded by bustle
music playing from the open church.
I hold on to her hand tighter
as we squeeze between stall tables and a party
of linen suits, rustling net.

Dazzle and light buzzes over the square,
the ice cream parlour, café tables, vendors and strollers
– all caught up in the performance.
The brides are beacons, white fragile layers waft around them.

We stand for a moment looking for the grooms,
men with winged collars dashing between sets of relations.
Or are they the stationary men off to one side
waiting for the brides to gather their trains
and settle their wide hoops in the backseats.

One bride, beautifully shod
steps concentratedly into the car; there's a rush of flowers,
guests carrying huge bouquets.

Almost at the edge now we make for clear space,
as if released from some great effort we step outside
the mothers' hopes, the fathers' pride.
With our good wishes, we watch the brides go.

In the Old Town

Give us this day, cobbles worn to shine like water
skin of walls lined and bleached
– sundown orange, smoky pink.
Lead us through narrow serpentine streets,
clothes draping balconies like banners
swifts dart round the roof tops, ricocheting calls.

Lead us into the thick of it, make a friend of time,
let our measure be light.
The first bite of a peach floods our fingers,
on earth as if we were in heaven.

For this is noon, the sea in earshot.
You halt and drift with the market crowd,
the space between us contoured, roofed with an awning.
When all your face comes into view
amid vendors' calls, in this ecstatic southern light
in all lights, as it was in our beginning,
you were the woman who drew me closer.

Unshowered, wrestling with the sea still on our skin
when she catches me, mid-room, with a kiss.
Not a passing glance of lips, but her intended
till I press back against the wall
laughing, in a body-search pose
as ready as her to forget about dinner.

Once, in our first months, we headed down Christopher Street
starch wafting from an open laundry, the sound of a press
squeezing a line along a sleeve. We slipped
across the West Side Highway, out on the pier
pressing our faces to the fence to catch an air of sea,
distant Liberty. Winter sun pouring its heart out
over the Hudson, she stepped into me –
the cold became a memory
smudged under our winter coats.

Two guys stood on the far side of the pier
looking baffled, how long they'd been there
god knows. Gulping, knees undone, we surfaced like swimmers
and almost ran back up Christopher Street
laughing. We'd been gone an hour, the night had come
there were shelves of lights up and down the tall streets,
she was all over me. Everything had turned on.

TOGETHER

We came down the path this morning.
Under the mountains now she is resting
lengthwise, with her shades on.

As I swim across the small bay
schools of fish silver below me
in and out of sun-bars. They come
through swaying boughs of weed, pulsing like neon.

My lungs squeeze me back,
back to the mountains' sudden rise,
after-sighting of the fish tickling below me.

There in her own element
she has spread herself beautifully,
tilted a little to the book she's reading,
covered in lotion, she's making the sun dance.

Cicadas ratcheting down to the bay,
polished scales of the olive trees.
With her there has always been vivid
affinity, now the mountains and the fish
– all under the wand of the sun
join in the yes and the shine.

WAITOHI

Seven poems in memory of Richard Pearse

A MAN FROM THE BACKBLOCKS

We were doing the pioneers.
They'd come from England with horses and linen,
pianos and tea, rowed from the ships
to the bay. They cleared the bush
from the coast back to the foothills
and the land was fenced into squares.

Overcast photographs of men in boaters,
braces, and waistcoats, and the women
in wide hooped skirts – dressed
for a rose garden in the middle of a muddy
backyard. Starched, all backbone,
as if they weren't looking at a camera
but a frontier – hard and hostile and bare.

There were dates and wars and more immigrations
and almost lost in the noise
of that lesson – a man who had lived
out in the backblocks, wanted to fly.

Richard William Pearse (1877–1953)

Born in the small farming settlement of Waitohi (South Is., NZ). A self-taught back-
yard mechanic who built his own aircraft and accomplished a powered take-off in
March 1903. It wasn't till after his death that Pearse's attempts to fly created any inter-
est outside his home district. He died in Sunnyside, a psychiatric hospital on the out-
skirts of Christchurch, NZ.

Young Inventor

When he was a boy he fashioned things
– springs and sprockets and the little fly wheels
in the back of clocks. Shy.
He fitted in and out of the gangs,
the team, family, but wire to wheel
wheel to rod connections spun like the planets.
The right fit was heaven. You could get into his world
through a diagram. The way the air drew him,
the way an element can sing to the right listener.

GROUNDING

Pasture fanned to the foot of the hills.
Fence-tamed. Land he was born to
at the time when the Wool Kings reigned.
He schooled himself in making do
– magazines mailed from America
on science and mechanics and astronomy.
He wrapped the reins around his neck
and held the book before him as he ploughed.
Plodding furrows. Above him blue acres of sky
– sometimes he could almost hear
cord of the wing on a cross-wind.

His fences sagged, his hedges grew delinquent,
and each year found him more alone than the last.

They believed the devil had got into him
– cutting down sheep-dip tins to make a propeller
and, behind the propeller, golden syrup cans
hammered and flattened and soldered together.

Weird sounds neighbours heard over his hedges.
And with the sight of him
biking back from the station, loaded
with bundles of bamboo and coils of wire
they gave, as if in his honour, the name 'mad Pearse',
crank, crazed, screw-loose – they downed
tools to watch the spectacle
as he knotted and pulleyed on a wind's incline.
When all held in its bamboo frame,
when the whole bric-à-brac, tin, stitched
salvaged thing bore like a harmony
over the fence lines. His reed-framed machine,
sailing on its calico.

SECOND SON

His father's sky was simply rain or shine
– his hands kept feeling for the horizon.
Could he have been a different son?

He drew lines in the air. The sound of air,
shifting its weight transported him.
'We weren't born with wings,' his father said.
Nothing to burn or fence – the sky
was a vacancy made for travel.
But in that back country he'd soon know –
no one believes you till you're dead.
Right from the start and through all the years
he'd been flying in the dark.

LAST ROOM

The sad inventory it made – a cot bed, a gas stove,
food in cans. Solo and makeshift,
gridding out lines of his aerial plans, working
on patents. The periphery his country.

Under that wide blue swimming-pool sky
years from the limelight he made
his swaying first flight, that slither of ecstasy
on the edge of the bird-zone.
Yet it was as if he'd never left the ground
so tightly did the walls wrap around him.

Nothing of value was found but the sloping shoulders
and shallow ribs of an instrument he kept by him. The room
was as silent as his old cello. His wings were trapped inside.

WAITOHI

The hills give and lean in opposition,
the echo of contact – green
and the paper lightness of summer.
The wind tasking, the wavy footsteps
of heat crossing paddocks. Velocities.
The grass on bended knee,
the electricities of a cabbage tree.

Up in the air, and gullies, troughs,
hill-line drafts. The twilight
sweeping from wing-tip to wing-tip.

★ ★ ★

HERON

The birds — at first we turned them
into a notion of mind. It was our thought
that took flight
— journeying up through ether
to stars, heaven, sun.
As if on the first rung
in the ladder of the air, the birds flew
and knew what the inside of a cloud looked like.

I stand under their flight path,
the gulls and rooks
and those crazy small swallows,
beating the hell out of the air.
But it's the heron, ever since childhood,
that has filled me with superstition
— standing at the water's edge
with great unbird-like stillness.

And to watch a heron fly
it's hard to believe
that the air doesn't hold it.
Stretching its wings out
in a long, slow bend
as if gravity were a soft bed.
The heron falls back against the sky
drifting like a sleeper when the dream is good.

THE ANNUNCIATION

Tintoretto

This is no swallow, no butterfly.
Feathered with Concorde power
Titanic bulk, breathlessly aerobic
Gabriel dives in under the lintel,
wings swept back behind Olympic shoulders
he tilts like a display pilot
and just clears the entrance.

Mary pulls up under the impact
cherubs sail on the draught
like a herd of sky-diving babies. Outside
Joseph grapples with a bit
of four by two, oblivious to the super-human
frequency. The earth's in a bad way.

As to Gabriel
you can see he's not going to help
pick up the pieces, he's not even going to land,
message delivered on a rush of air,
no buttering up of Mary,
his beautiful arms poised towards heaven
before he back-flips out of there.

THE OLD RAILWAY TRACK

(Finsbury Park to Highgate)

I

I walk on the narrow where the rails once ran.
The dark months browning out
in the last of the leaf mould.
As if this is what the freight trains promised
rumbling on the edge of my girlhood sleep.
I'm waking in another country.
The cherry trees switched on over night,
delicate and surprising as snow,
buttercup and campion. The blossom
swirling up like a Japanese cloud.

II

Bricks of the old railway tunnel, once stained with engines,
are now a cave of tags and blurs.
The boys shake out their spray cans, colours loop
and ride, the walls themselves come back to life.
Beyond their fumes and gallery
the lines have started tapping, juice of cog and wheel.
As I press against a single tree
young woodland comes within my ear, the draw of roots,
and up above new finger tips of green.
Scripts like jazz or kung fu. The dereliction broken.

III

The only transport now is with the wind
– transfers of energy, trees in gentle motion.
I walk along the trackbed
as if between two lands of thought
her hand absently
arriving into my hand, and then this hour
that's just beyond her leaving,
this gap before the night comes down.
She is in air space, between countries,
and I'm neither here nor there.
Heavens above, what glows the twilight has!
As if the trees themselves were taking off.

COROT'S TREES

On the anniversary of my mother's death

In the Southern Hemisphere mists were few,
wide blues of sky,
each tree stood up on the plains.
Tips of a pine, the packed-in leaves
of a poplar – planted along fence lines
to stop the wind.

Yet she might have known this other country
in which the trees stand like dreamers,
unemployed. The times she paused,
inclined like the sketched-in figure of the woman
who stretches her arms into the boughs
for a child, a fruit, a letter.

Purpose hidden, all the reasons brown.
And while the trees lose all their detail,
the summer holds
in the soft clothing Corot gave his distances.
How a past is stored. She kept the print
on the best wall for years,
the great mirrors of the lake resting
one version against another, in her memory.

The boarding lounge view from the windows magnetic with sun,
Manukau harbour stretches away from the runways
– the water looks beautifully strong, it pulls against me.

The distance is something I can never believe
as the gates close. The plane becomes a third hemisphere,
shielded from the outside, mountains that I look down into,
contour lines wiggling against each other like so many horizons.

The big surf hushed, the plane nosing into its climb, waves height
turns to a finger-line slowly tracing down the island's side,
etching inside me, even the clouds feel indigenous
like belongings I keep leaving behind but love.